Road Trip: Exploring America's Regions

LET'S EXPLORE THE NORTHEAST

BY KATHLEEN CONNORS

Gareth Stevens
Publishing

Please visit our website, www.garethstevens.com. For a free color catalog of all our high-quality books, call toll free 1-800-542-2595 or fax 1-877-542-2596.

Library of Congress Cataloging-in-Publication Data

Connors, Kathleen.
  Let's explore the Northeast / Kathleen Connors.
      pages cm. — (Road trip: exploring America's regions)
  Includes index.
  ISBN 978-1-4339-9135-6 (pbk.)
  ISBN 978-1-4339-9136-3 (6-pack)
  ISBN 978-1-4339-9134-9 (library binding)
  1. Northeastern States–Juvenile literature. I. Title. II. Title: Let us explore the Northeast.
  F4.3.C66 2013
  917.404'44—dc23
                                          2012049132

First Edition

Published in 2014 by
Gareth Stevens Publishing
111 East 14th Street, Suite 349
New York, NY 10003

Copyright © 2014 Gareth Stevens Publishing

Designer: Andrea Davison-Bartolotta
Editor: Kristen Rajczak

Photo credits: Cover, p. 1 (left) iStockphoto/Thinkstock, (right) Marianne Campolongo/Shutterstock.com; cover, backcover, interior backgrounds (texture) Marilyn Volan/Shutterstock.com; cover, backcover (map) Stacey Lynne Payne/ Shutterstock.com; cover, backcover, pp. 1, 22–24 (green sign) Shutterstock.com; interior backgrounds (road) Renata Novackova/Shutterstock.com, (blue sign) Vitezslav Valka/Shutterstock.com; pp. 4, 5 (map), 7, 13 (state outline), 17 (yellow note), 21 iStockphoto/Thinkstock; p. 5 (curled corner) JonnyDrake/Shutterstock.com, (background) Richard Cavalleri/Shutterstock.com; p. 8 ExaMedia Photography/Shutterstock.com; p. 9 dibrova/Shutterstock.com; p. 11 Michael Ivins/Boston Red Sox/Getty Images; p. 12 spirit of america/Shutterstock.com; p. 13 AridOcean/Shutterstock.com; p. 14 philhawley/Shutterstock.com; p. 15 Leighton O'Connor Jr./Shutterstock.com; p. 17 (left) jreika/Shutterstock.com, (right) Lifesize/Thinkstock; p. 19 (top left) Luke Frazza/AFP/Getty Images, (top right) Hulton Archive/Getty Images, (bottom left) Express/Express/Getty Images, (bottom right) Mark Mainz/Getty Images; p. 20 Bradley C. Bower/Bloomberg via Getty Images.

Printed in the United States of America

CPSIA compliance information: Batch #CS13GS: For further information contact Gareth Stevens, New York, New York at 1-800-542-2595.

Contents

Words in the glossary appear in **bold** type the first time they are used in the text.

A Historic Region

Of all the **regions** in the United States, the Northeast may be the one most tied to our nation's beginnings. The first shots of the **American Revolution** rang out at the Battles of Lexington and Concord in Massachusetts. The Declaration of Independence was signed in Philadelphia, Pennsylvania. The whole region was part of the 13 original US states.

With historic battlefields, big cities, and rugged mountains, the Northeast is full of fantastic places to visit.

The Northeast

The Northeast

at a Glance

	State	Population (2010)	Date of Statehood	Capital	State Bird	State Flower
1	**Connecticut**	3,574,097	Jan. 9, 1788	Hartford	American robin	mountain laurel
2	**Maine**	1,328,361	March 15, 1820	Augusta	black-capped chickadee	white pine cone and tassel
3	**Massachusetts**	6,547,629	Feb. 6, 1788	Boston	black-capped chickadee and wild turkey	mayflower
4	**New Hampshire**	1,316,470	June 21, 1788	Concord	purple finch	purple lilac and pink lady's slipper
5	**New Jersey**	8,791,894	Dec. 18, 1787	Trenton	eastern goldfinch	blue violet
6	**New York**	19,378,102	July 26, 1788	Albany	eastern bluebird	rose
7	**Pennsylvania**	12,702,379	Dec. 12, 1787	Harrisburg	ruffed grouse	mountain laurel
8	**Rhode Island**	1,052,567	May 29, 1790	Providence	Rhode Island red chicken	blue violet
9	**Vermont**	625,741	March 4, 1791	Montpelier	hermit thrush	red clover

All Seasons

When talking about the Northeast, it's often said: "If you don't like the weather, wait a minute." Nearness to the ocean and the many lakes around the region often cause quick weather changes. In general, though, the Northeast has four seasons.

Bodies of water cause differences in **precipitation**, too—even across a state. During the winter of 2010–2011 Syracuse, New York, saw 179 inches (455 cm) of snow. About 250 miles (400 km) away, New York City saw only about 62 inches (157 cm) of snow.

The Northeast can have very cold winters. In Vermont, known as a great place to ski, temperatures can reach below −34°F (−37°C)!

A Bite of the Big Apple

New York City is the largest city in the United States. It's so big, it has two **professional** teams in each of three sports: football, baseball, and basketball. While exciting events like a Yankees game or Broadway play make the city a great road-trip **destination**, it's also important internationally. New York City is where the **United Nations** is headquartered.

Tourists can also visit both Ellis Island and the Statue of Liberty by **ferry**. Here, visitors can learn the stories of **immigrants** finding hope when coming to our country.

Statue of Liberty

Almost 8.2 million people live in New York City—and that's not counting the large number of tourists visiting the city at any given time!

Pit Stop

The Hudson River runs right through New York City. Tourists often take night cruises on the river to see the city's skyscrapers light up.

City Side Trips

Home to more than 1.5 million people, Philadelphia, Pennsylvania, is the fifth-largest US city. Independence Hall, where the US Constitution was written, is in the heart of the city. The famous steps from the movie *Rocky* are in downtown Philly, too. They're an entrance to the Philadelphia Museum of Art.

In Boston, Massachusetts, visitors can learn about history up close at the historic sites of the Boston **Massacre** and the Boston Tea Party. They can also take a walk through the campus of Harvard University!

Pit Stop

With so many historic places in Boston, it's hard to see them all! The Freedom Trail walking tour guides visitors through the city so they can see many, including the Bunker Hill Monument and the USS *Constitution* in Boston Harbor.

Boston is the third-largest city in the Northeast and the 21st-largest city in the United States. Fenway Park, home to the Boston Red Sox, is a ballpark many baseball fans travel to.

11

The Mighty Appalachians

Big cities aren't the only road-trip destinations in the Northeast! The Appalachians are some of Earth's oldest mountains. Part of this range, the Green Mountains, towers over Vermont, and the White Mountains rise above New Hampshire. The Appalachians wind through New York, Massachusetts, Connecticut, and Pennsylvania, and continue south, too.

The many parts of the Appalachians in the Northeast are fun to visit for camping, hiking, and skiing. Many people hike parts of the Appalachian Trail, which begins in Maine and ends in Georgia.

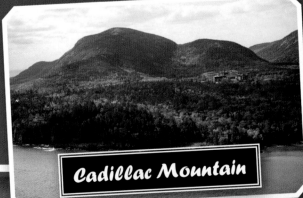

Cadillac Mountain

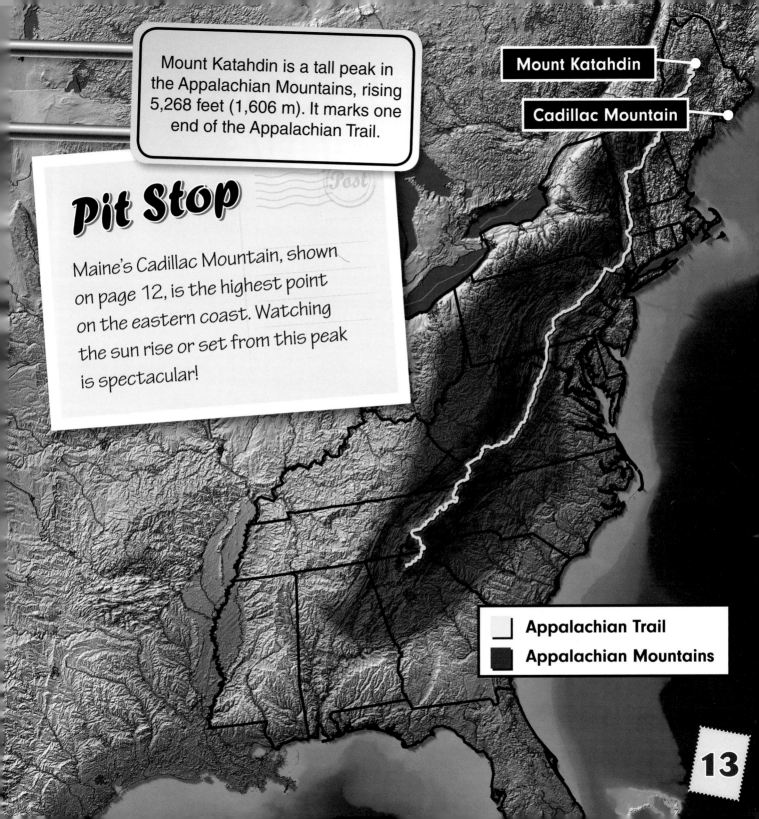

Mount Katahdin is a tall peak in the Appalachian Mountains, rising 5,268 feet (1,606 m). It marks one end of the Appalachian Trail.

Mount Katahdin

Cadillac Mountain

Pit Stop

Maine's Cadillac Mountain, shown on page 12, is the highest point on the eastern coast. Watching the sun rise or set from this peak is spectacular!

Appalachian Trail
Appalachian Mountains

Visiting the Waterways

From the Hudson River to Massachusetts Bay, the bodies of water in the Northeast played a big role in its settlement. They were sources of food and transportation. Today, many people just like to vacation on their shores!

Some waterways act as natural borders between states. The Delaware River divides Pennsylvania and New Jersey. Lake Champlain splits New York and Vermont.

Pit Stop

Called one of the seven wonders of the natural world, Niagara Falls is located between New York State and Ontario, Canada. Visitors can view the huge waterfall from either side of the border!

The many bodies of water in the Northeast are sources of fun for both those who live there and visitors. If you're in Newport, Rhode Island, you might catch a boat race in Narragansett Bay!

15

Oceanside

Every state in the Northeast except Pennsylvania touches the Atlantic Ocean. Cape Cod, Massachusetts; Bar Harbor, Maine; and Atlantic City, New Jersey, are some of the most popular coastal spots.

Surrounded by Acadia National Park, Bar Harbor is a great place for nature lovers, hikers, and mountain bikers. The first Atlantic City Boardwalk was built in 1870. In 2012, Hurricane Sandy destroyed much of the historic walk. The storm was so strong, it washed away big parts of the boardwalk as it pounded the coast.

Pit Stop

Many places along the coasts of Massachusetts and Maine, including Bar Harbor and Cape Cod, offer whale-watching trips. Travelers board a boat and ride the waves of the Atlantic to try to spot whales, dolphins, and fish.

Post

New England Clam Chowder

Ingredients:

4 slices bacon, chopped
1 1/2 cups chopped onion
1 1/2 cups water
4 cups peeled and chopped potatoes
1 1/2 tsp salt
3 cups half-and-half
3 tbsp butter
2 10-ounce cans minced clams

Directions:

1. Cook bacon in a large pot until almost crispy.

2. Add onions to the pot and cook them for about 5 minutes.

3. Stir in water, potatoes, and salt. Bring the mixture to a boil and cook for 15 minutes, uncovered.

4. Stir in half-and-half and butter.

5. Open cans of clams and drain, saving the liquid from the cans.

6. Stir in clams and half of the liquid from the cans.

7. Let heat in pot for about 5 minutes, but don't boil.

The Northeast coast is known for its seafood. Ask for an adult's help, and follow these steps to make your own New England clam chowder.

Famous Northeasterners

From Massachusetts-born presidents John F. Kennedy and George H. W. Bush to Maine-based author Stephen King, the Northeast has been home to many famous Americans.

Have you ever seen the painting, *32 Campbell's Soup Cans?* American artist Andy Warhol painted it! Warhol was born in Pittsburgh, Pennsylvania. He made his mark on modern art from the 1950s to the 1980s. You can see his colorful paintings, sculptures, videos, and other work at the Warhol Museum in Pittsburgh.

Pit Stop

Learn more about President Kennedy at the John F. Kennedy Presidential Library and Museum in Boston. One display allows you to experience the sights and sounds of his presidential run.

George H. W. Bush

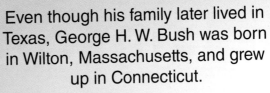

Even though his family later lived in Texas, George H. W. Bush was born in Wilton, Massachusetts, and grew up in Connecticut.

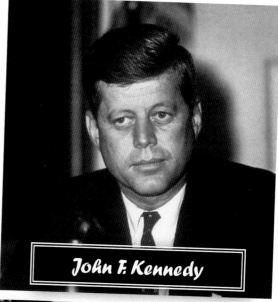

John F. Kennedy

Andy Warhol

Stephen King

The Fun Starts Here

In addition to the majestic mountains and historic places, the Northeast is home to some of the best-known—and most fun—companies in our nation. You can visit the home of Ben and Jerry's Ice Cream in Waterbury, Vermont, and try out new flavors on a factory tour. Hershey, Pennsylvania, offers another tasty stop: Hershey's Chocolate World.

Do you like to color with crayons? In Easton, Pennsylvania, visitors to the Crayola Experience can learn about the Crayola Company in full color!

Beautiful Views in the Northeast

Pine Tree State Arboretum

Thousand Islands

Finger Lakes

Flume Gorge

Kancamagus Highway

Glossary

American Revolution: the war in which the colonies won their freedom from England

destination: the place someone is traveling to

ferry: a boat used to carry passengers or goods

immigrant: someone who moves from one country to another to live

massacre: the cruel killing of a large number of people

precipitation: rain, snow, sleet, or hail

professional: earning money from an activity that many people do for fun

region: an area

tourist: a person traveling to visit a place

United Nations: a group of nations that united after World War II with the intention of resolving conflicts between nations

For More Information

Books

Franchino, Vicky. *It's Cool to Learn About the United States: Northeast.* Ann Arbor, MI: Cherry Lake Publishing, 2012.

Greil, Marlene. *United States, the Land.* New York, NY: Crabtree Publishing Co., 2012.

Rau, Dana Meachen. *The Northeast.* New York, NY: Children's Press, 2012.

Websites

Northeast Region
www.nps.gov/nero/kids/#
Use the National Park Service website to find out about the junior ranger program as well as where national parks and historic sites are around the Northeast region.

States and Regions
www.harcourtschool.com/ss1/adventure_activities/grade4.html
Use this interactive website to learn more about the regions of the United States.

Index